D0641176

DO YOU KNOW

Porcupines?

Written by
Alain M. Bergeron
Michel Quintin
Sampar

Illustrations by
Sampar

Translated by
Solange Messier

Fitzhenry & Whiteside

Published in Canada by Fitzhenry & Whiteside, 195 Allstate Parkway,
Markham, Ontario L3R 4T8
Published in the United States by Fitzhenry & Whiteside, 311 Washington Street, Brighton, Massachusetts 02135

www.fitzhenry.ca godwit@fitzhenry.ca

10 9 8 7 6 5 4 3 2 1

Library and Archives Canada Cataloguing in Publication
Do You Know Crows?
ISBN 978-1-55455-321-1 (pbk.)
Data available on file

Publisher Cataloging-in-Publication Data (U.S.)
Bergeron, Alain M.
Do you know porcupines?/ Alain M. Bergeron ; Michel Quintin ; illustrations by Sampar ;
translated by Solange Messier.
Originally published in French as: Savais-tu? les porcs-épics; Waterloo, Quebec: Éditions Michel Quintin, 2011.
[64] p. : col. ill. ; cm.
Summary: Fascinating and informative facts about porcupines presented in graphic novel format.
ISBN: 978-1-55455-321-1 (pbk.)
1. Porcupines – Juvenile literature. I. Quintin, Michel. II. Sampar. III. Messier, Solange. IV. Title.
599.35/97 dc23   QL737.R652.B374 2013

Fitzhenry & Whiteside acknowledges with thanks the Canada Council for the Arts, and the Ontario Arts Council for their support of our publishing program. We acknowledge the financial support of the Government of Canada through the Canada Book Fund (CBF) for our publishing activities.

Cover and text design by Daniel Choi
Cover image by Sampar
Printed in Canada by Friesens Corporation

MIX
Paper from responsible sources
FSC® C016245

More than 20 porcupine **species** exist. They can be found in the New World (Americas) as well as in the Old World (Africa, Asia and Europe).

Porcupine fur is made up of hair and quills. The quills, which are absent on the porcupine's snout, the interior of its legs, and its belly, are actually hairs modified to form rigid thorns.

A porcupine's **predators**, which are few, kill it by either biting its head or flipping it over to attack its belly.

The porcupine has the longest quills of all land animals. Some species, like the crested porcupine, have quills that can measure up to 50 centimetres (19.6 in) in length.

These **mammals** are among the biggest **rodents** in the world. The North American porcupine can weigh up to 18 kilograms (39.6 lbs) while the crested porcupine can weigh up to 27 kilograms (59.5 lbs).

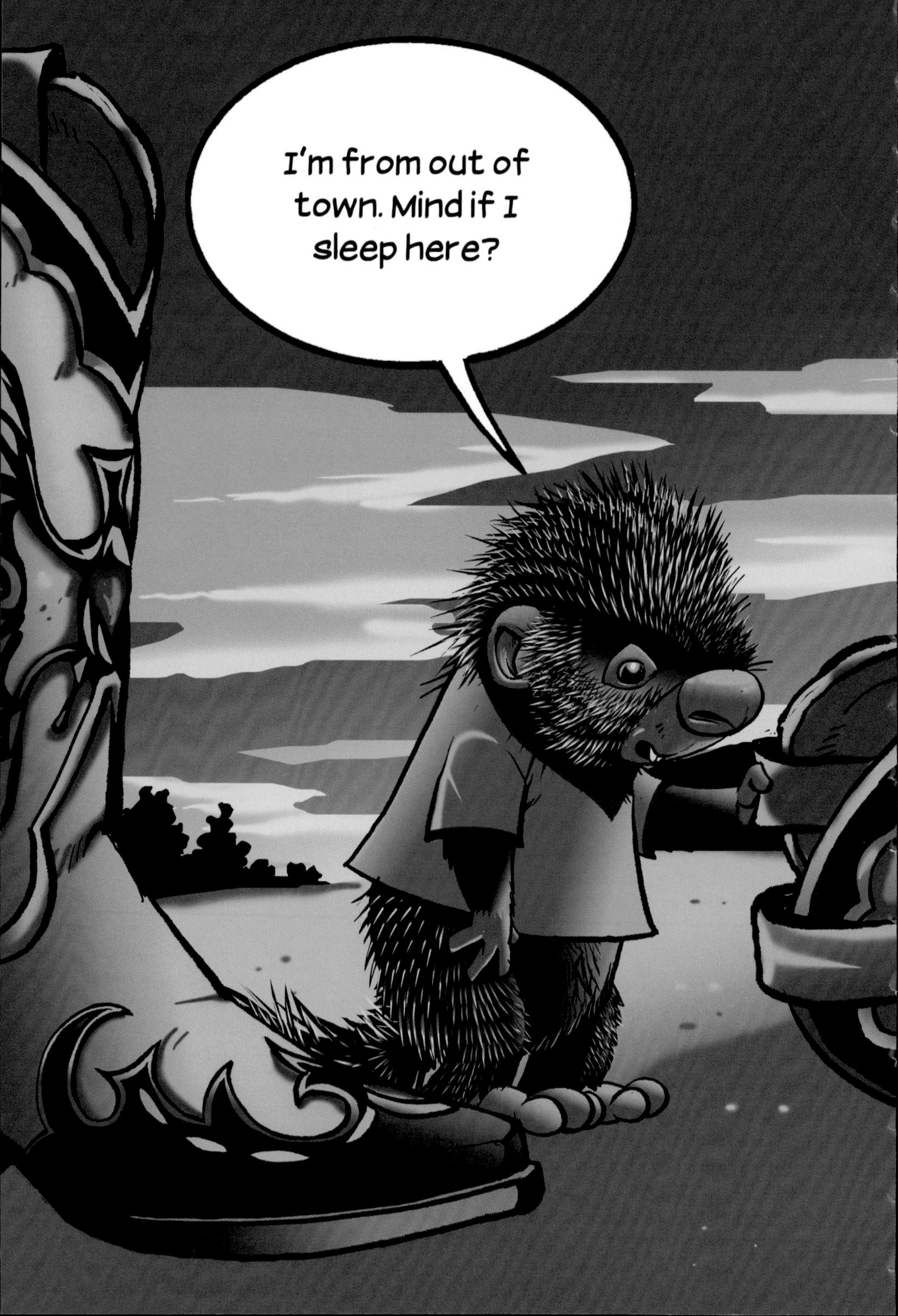
I'm from out of town. Mind if I sleep here?

Other species, like the Bahia porcupine, are smaller, weighing less than 1 kilogram (2.2 lbs).

Porcupines live in forests, prairies and deserts. They are **nocturnal** animals.

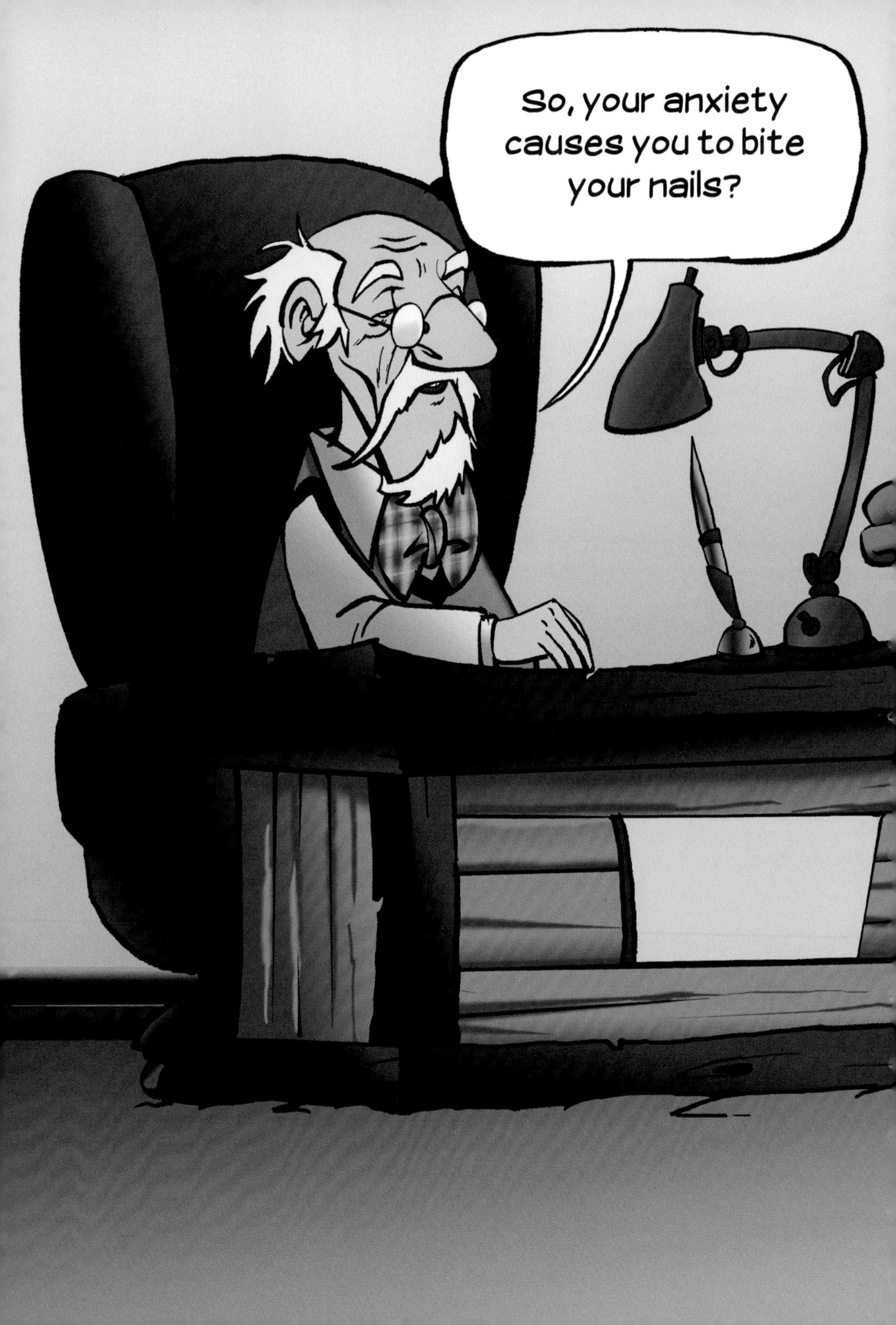
So, your anxiety causes you to bite your nails?

These rodents possess four prominent **incisors** that grow continuously and are always sharp.

A porcupine's predators include bobcats, cougars, lynx, bears and fishers (a type of weasel).

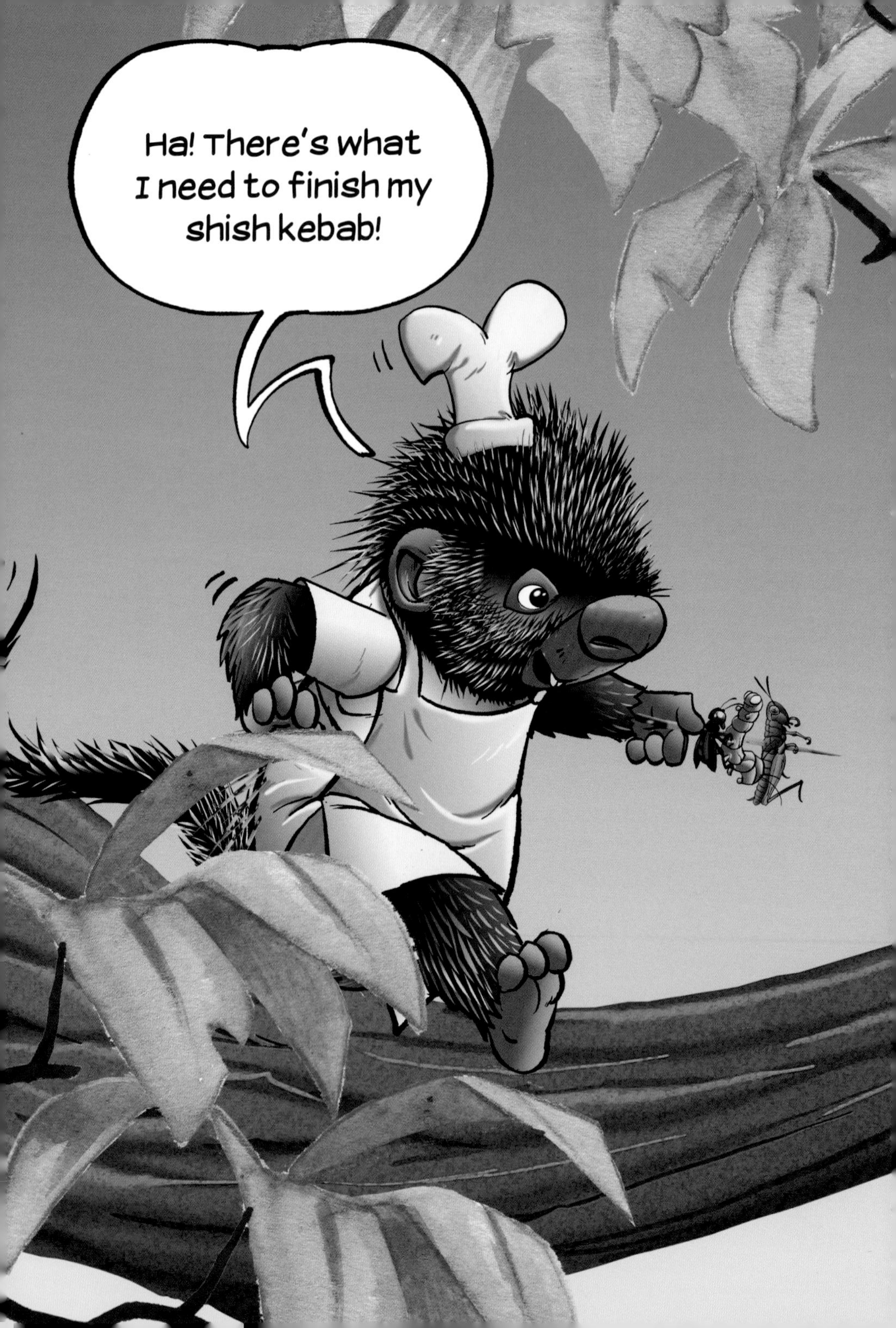
Ha! There's what I need to finish my shish kebab!

As **vegetarians**, porcupines eat leaves, plant buds, small fruits and some types of tree bark. Some species, like the **prehensile-tailed** porcupine, also eat insects and small reptiles.

Porcupines love salt. They'll gnaw on anything that contains salt, like bones of dead animals and shed deer antlers. That's why they'll also eat things covered with urine or sweat.

Because they also lick the salt off of roads, porcupines often get hit by automobiles.

A porcupine's quills help it float while swimming.

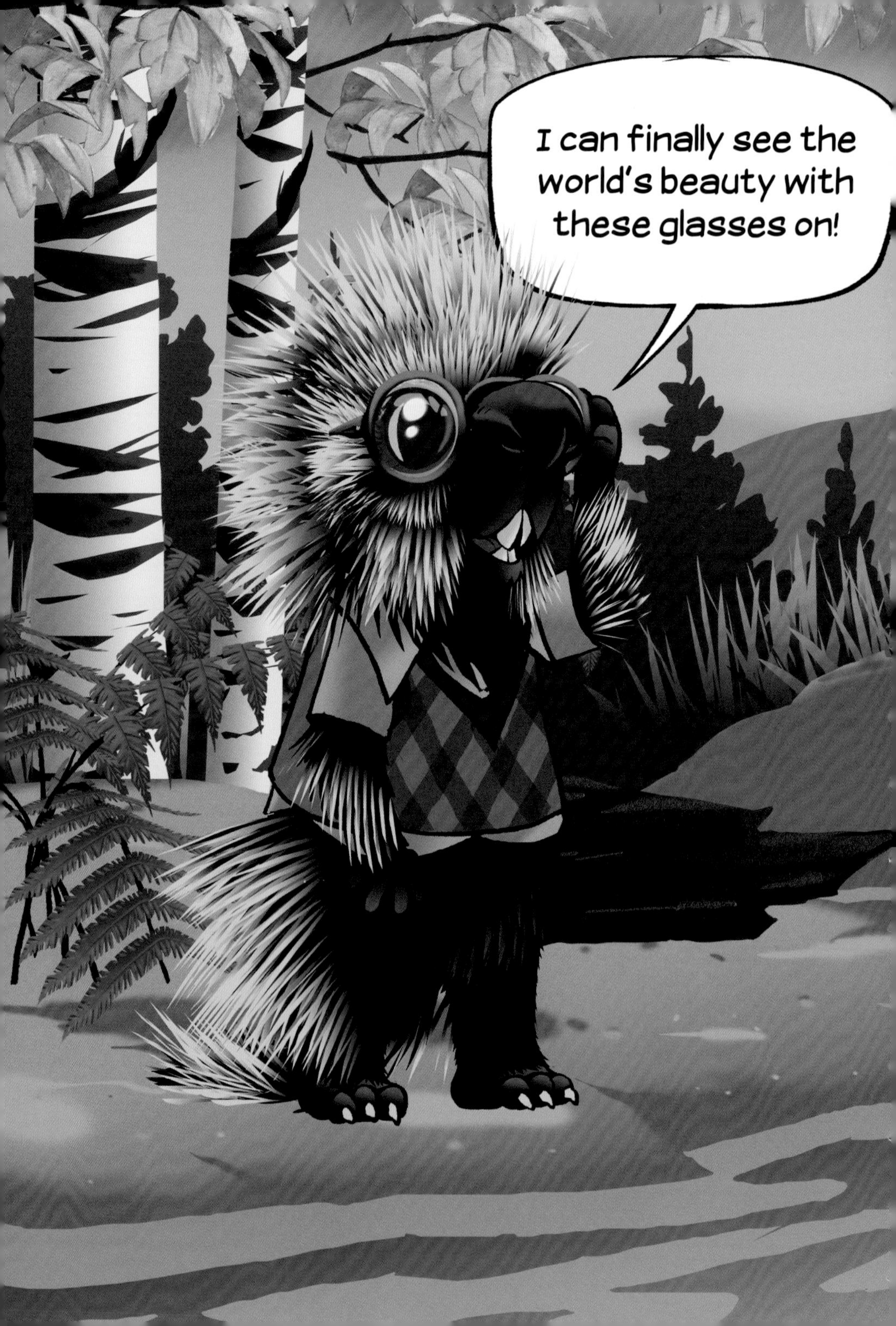
I can finally see the world's beauty with these glasses on!

Porcupines can't see very well since they are **nearsighted**. However, they have excellent hearing and a great sense of smell.

Porcupines emit all sorts of sounds: whines, moans, grunts, coughs, sharp cries, yelps and wails.

Sorry, little girl, I've heard lots of different sounds, but nothing that even remotely resembles a song. NEXT!
Judge

Because their quills are so sharp, porcupines must be very careful while mating.

To find out if a female is ready to mate, a North American porcupine will advance near her while grunting, stand on its hind legs and spray her with a powerful jet of urine.

If she's ready to mate, she'll let herself get completely drenched by the pee, otherwise, she'll forcefully shake it all off.

Porcupines usually only have one baby per birth. Twins are rare.

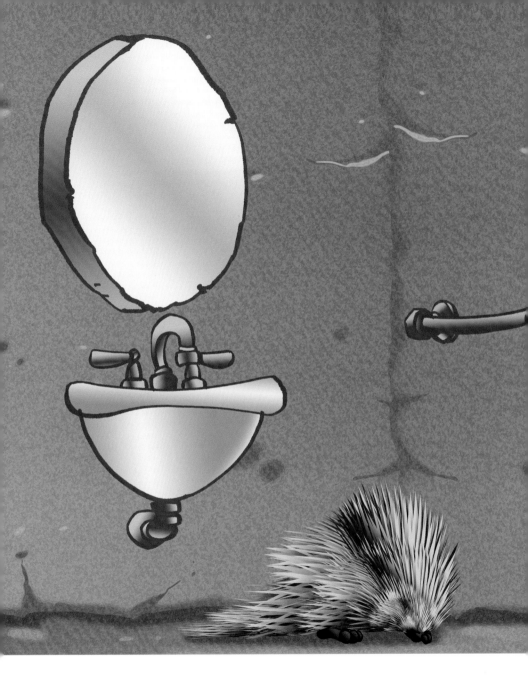

Right from birth, a baby porcupine can move around and open its eyes. By reflex, it already has a defensive attitude.

Porcupines are born covered in quills. The quills are soft at first but harden within a few hours.

The North American porcupine, also know as the Canadian porcupine, possesses approximately 30,000 quills.

The quills' tips are topped with little hooks that inflate when they penetrate the skin. That's what makes them so difficult to remove.

When porcupines feel threatened, they curl up in a ball and ruffle their quills. If they have to counter-attack, they'll move backwards or sideways while forcefully whipping their prickly tail back and forth.

Many people mistakenly think that porcupines can throw their quills. In fact, the quills are so lightly attached to their bodies that they fall off during contact.

When porcupines whip their tails around, for example, quills can become loose and give the impression that they are being thrown.

Quills can cause serious injuries and even death.

They can puncture a vital organ or be released into an aggressor's mouth, forcing the animal to starve to death.

All porcupines that live in the Americas are **arboreal**. These excellent climbers have long claws that help them easily scale trees.

Some species, like the prehensile-tailed porcupine, possess long tails devoid of quills that can be wrapped around branches.

Contrary to those that live in Europe, Africa and Asia, North American porcupines are **solitary** creatures.

I accidentally crushed it when I rubbed my back against the tree.

The North American porcupine is the only species you might meet north of Mexico and in Alaska. This animal is active year round.

Some porcupines can live for more than 20 years. One of the oldest known porcupines came from Malaysia. It lived to be 27 years old in captivity.

Glossary

Arboreal living in trees

Incisors front teeth adapted for gnawing and cutting

Mammal warm-blooded, back-boned animals

Nearsighted unable to see objects that are far away

Nocturnal active at night

Predator a hunter that kills prey for food

Prehensile tail a tail that can grasp or hold onto objects

Rodents gnawing mammals, which include mice, rats, and hamsters

Solitary living alone

Species a classification for a group of organisms with common characteristics

Vegetarian an animal that does not eat meat

Index

Do You Know there are other titles?

Rats

Crows

Crocodiles

Leeches

Chameleons

Toads

Spiders